HAL LEONARD PIANO REPERTOIRE
Book 1 · Elementary

JOURNEY THROUGH THE
CLASSICS

COMPILED AND EDITED BY JENNIFER LINN

Journey Through the Classics is a four-volume piano repertoire series designed to lead students seamlessly from the easiest classics to the intermediate masterworks. The graded pieces are presented in a progressive order and feature a variety of classical favorites essential to any piano student's educational foundation. The authentic repertoire is ideal for auditions and recitals and each book includes a handy reference chart with the key, composer, stylistic period, and challenge elements listed for each piece.

-Jennifer Linn

Dedicated in loving memory to my mother and first teacher,
Geraldine Ruth Ryan Lange.

Cover Art: Rose Garden, 1876 (oil on canvas) by Claude Monet (1840-1926)
Private Collection/ Photo © Lefevre Fine Art Ltd., London/ The Bridgeman Art Library
Nationality / copyright status: French / out of copyright
Adaptation by Jen McClellan

ISBN 978-4584-1149-5

7777 W. BLUEMOUND RD. P.O. BOX 13819 MILWAUKEE, WI 53213

In Australia Contact:
Hal Leonard Australia Pty. Ltd.
4 Lentara Court
Cheltenham, Victoria, 3192 Australia
Email: ausadmin@halleonard.com.au

Visit Hal Leonard Online at
www.halleonard.com

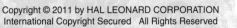

JOURNEY THROUGH THE CLASSICS:
Book 1 Reference Chart

✔ WHEN COMPLETED	PAGE	TITLE	COMPOSER	ERA	KEY	METER	CHALLENGE ELEMENTS
	4	RENAISSANCE DANCE	Praetorius	Baroque	C	4/4	Eighth notes & slurs
	5	FOLLOW THE LEADER	Köhler	Romantic	C	4/4	Eighth notes in imitation
	5	LITTLE MARCH	Türk	Classical	C	4/4	RH in treble C; eighth notes and slurs
	6	ALLEGRO	Reinagle	Classical	C	2/4	RH in treble C; 2-note slurs; D.C. al Fine
	7	VIVACE	Gurlitt	Romantic	C	4/4	RH in treble C; LH harmonic intervals
	8	THE BRAVE HORSEMAN	Vogel	Romantic	C	4/4	RH shift in treble; RH/LH coordination, syncopation
	9	HUNTING HORNS	Gurlitt	Romantic	C	4/4	Staccato; harmonic interval slurs
	10	CLASSIC MINUET	Linn	Classical	F	3/4	F major key signature; 6ths; 3/4 time signature
	11	ROMANCE	Wohlfahrt	Romantic	Dm	3/4	D minor key signature; dynamic control
	12	SHEPHERD'S FLUTE	Salutrinskaya	Romantic	Dm	4/4	D minor key signature; RH in 𝄢; damper pedal
	13	MINUET IN C	Hook	Classical	C	3/4	RH/LH coordination; triplet rhythm
	14	LYRICAL ETUDE	Beyer	Romantic	G	4/4	G major key signature; LH accompaniment & balance
	15	ETUDE IN G	Czerny	Classical	G	4/4	G major key signature; LH alberti bass
	16	THE PENNYWHISTLE	Türk	Romantic	G	4/4	C♯ accidental; RH/LH coordination
	17	PROCESSION	Reinagle	Classical	G	4/4	Staccato/legato coordination; hand shifts
	18	MINUET	Reinagle	Classical	C	3/4	RH hand shifts; staccato/legato coordination
	19	LITTLE BIRD	Gurlitt	Romantic	C	2/4	Both hands in 𝄞; staccato/legato coordination
	20	MELODY	Diabelli	Classical	C	4/4	Both hands in 𝄞; ties in LH voicing
	21	DANCE	Gurlitt	Romantic	C	3/4	Both hands in 𝄞; balance in melody/accompaniment
	22	ETUDE IN E MINOR	Gurlitt	Romantic	Em	4/4	E minor key signature; LH alberti bass
	24	LITTLE WALTZ	Gurlitt	Romantic	F	3/4	Balance in melody/accompaniment; hand shifts
	26	GAVOTTA	Hook	Classical	C	4/4	Staccato/legato coordination; dynamic echo
	28	BAGATELLE	Diabelli	Classical	G	3/4	LH harmonic intervals and 3-note chords
	29	BOURRÉE IN D MINOR	Graupner	Baroque	Dm	¢	D minor key signature, articulation & coordination
	30	MENUET EN RONDEAU	Rameau	Baroque	C	3/4	RH scale passages & contrapuntal skills

CONTENTS

4

Renaissance Dance

Michael Praetorius
(1571–1621)

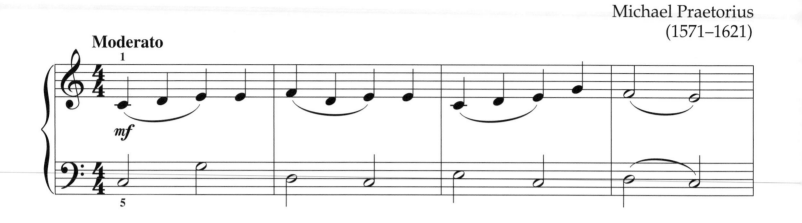

Follow the Leader

Louis Köhler
(1820–1886)

Little March

Daniel Gottlob Türk
(1750–1813)

Allegro

Alexander Reinagle
(1756–1809)

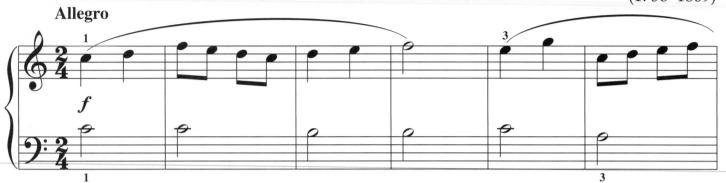

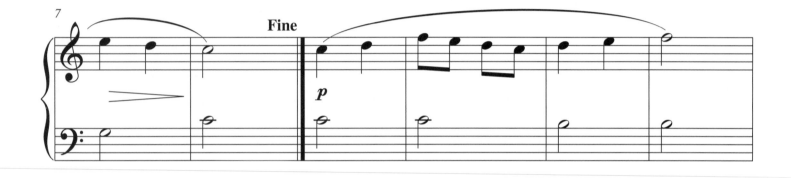

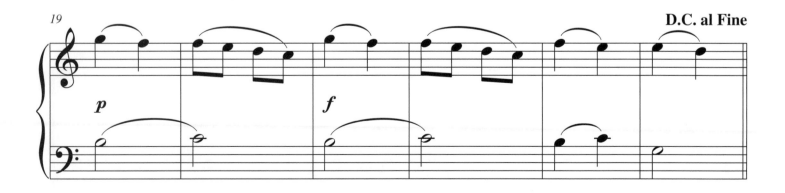

Vivace
Op. 117, No. 8

Cornelius Gurlitt
(1820–1901)

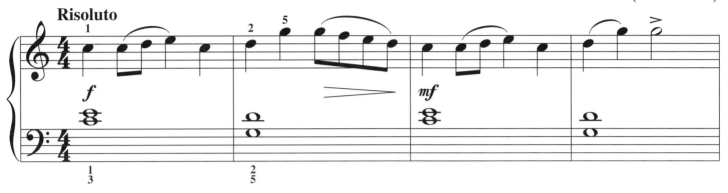

The Brave Horseman

Moritz Vogel
(1846–1922)

Marcia con forza

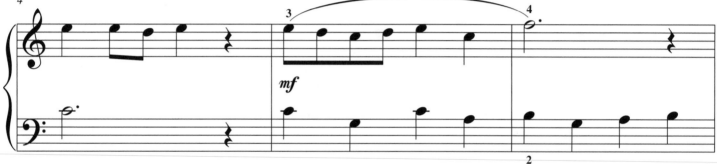

Hunting Horns
Op. 117, No. 10

Corneluis Gurlitt
(1820–1901)

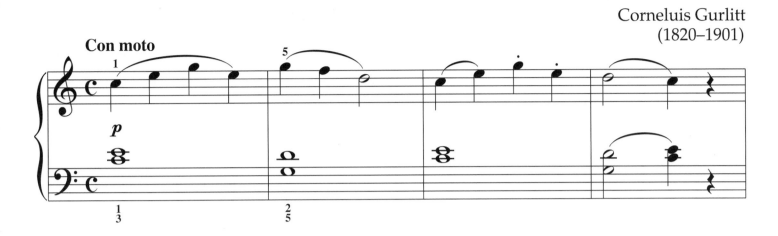

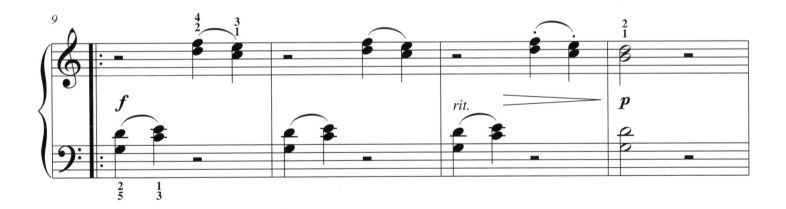

Classic Minuet

Jennifer Linn
(1960–)

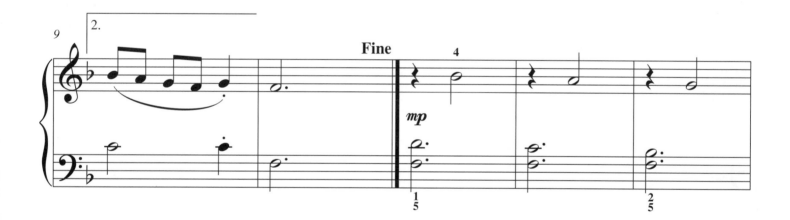

Romance

Heinrich Wohlfahrt
(1797–1883)

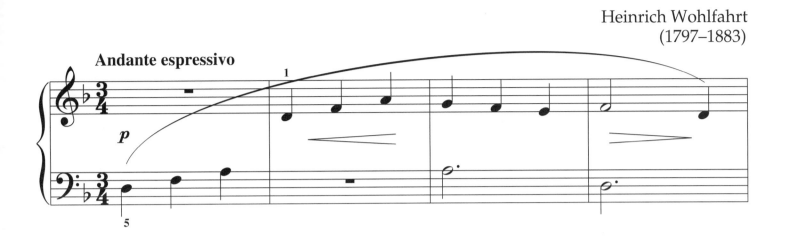

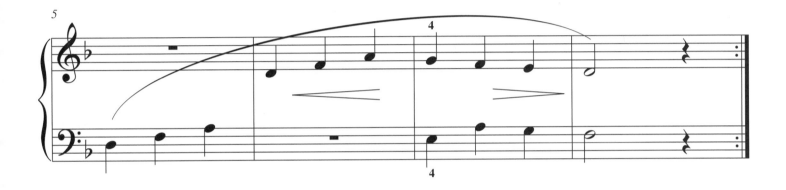

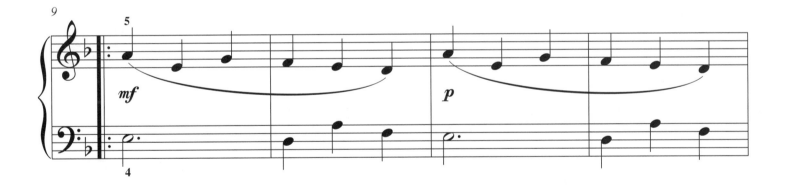

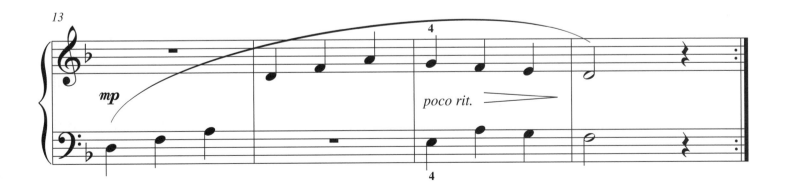

Shepherd's Flute

Tat'iana Salutrinskaya
(unknown)

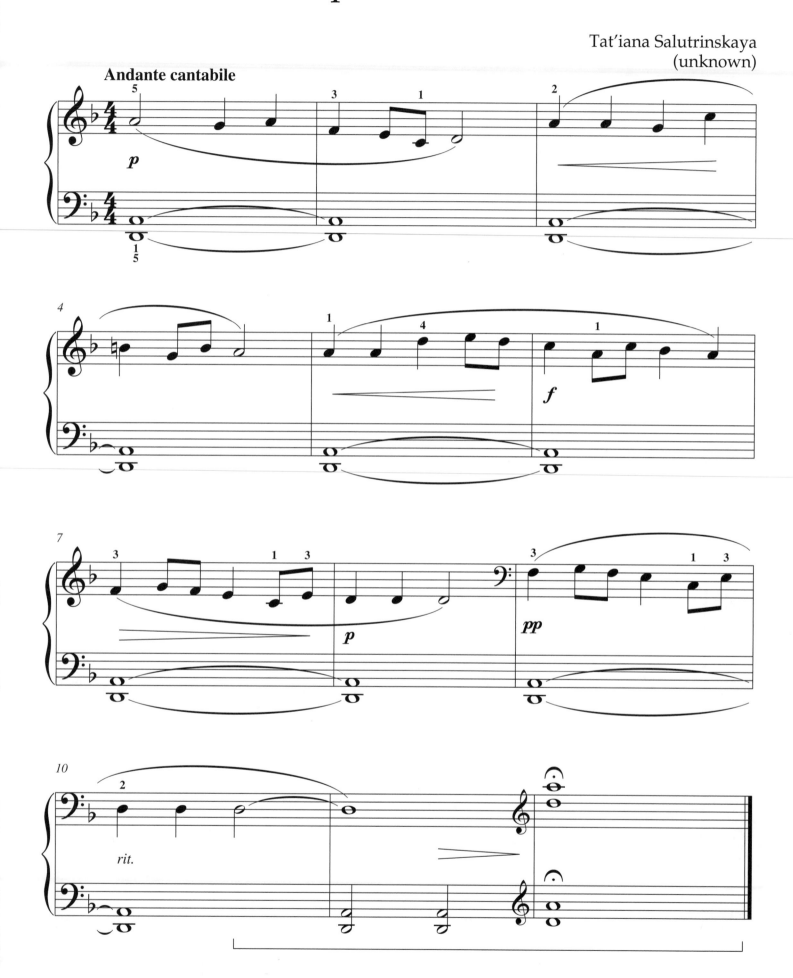

Minuet in C

James Hook
(1746–1827)

Moderato

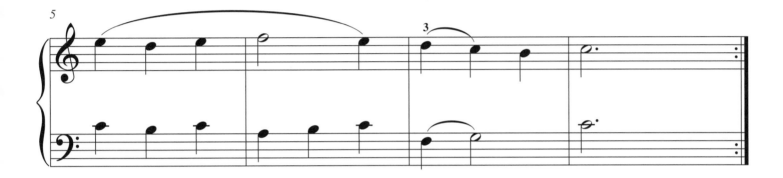

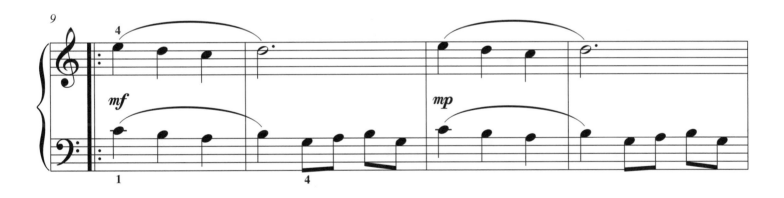

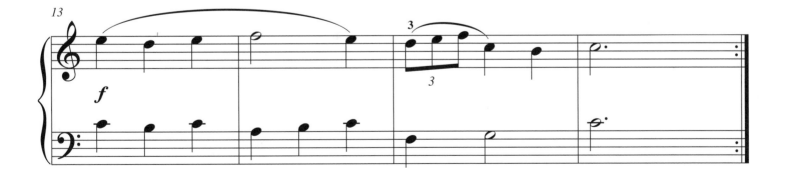

Lyrical Etude
Op. 101, No. 39

Ferdinand Beyer
(1803–1863)

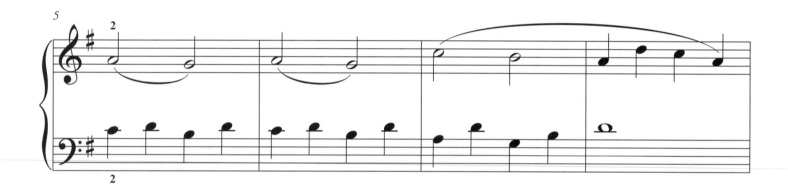

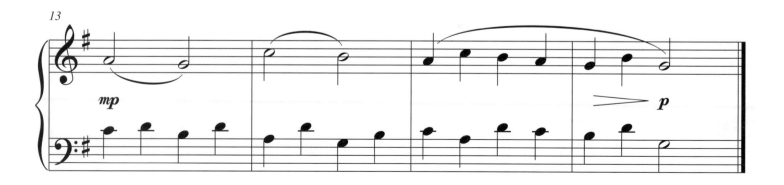

Etude in G
Op. 823, No. 11

Carl Czerny
(1791–1857)

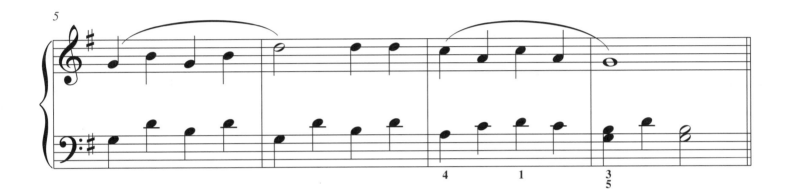

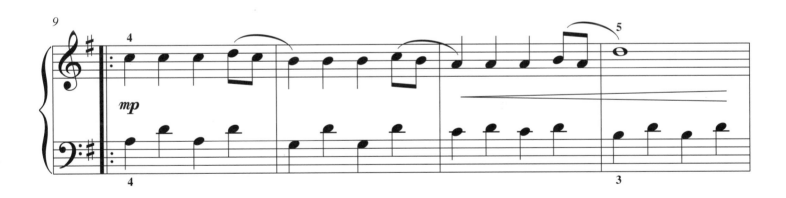

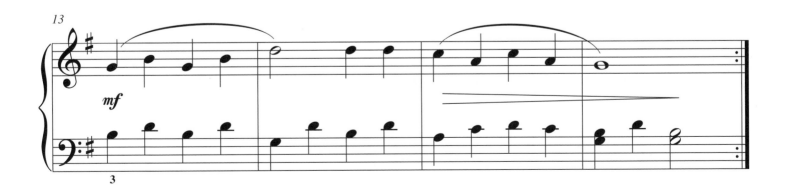

The Pennywhistle

Daniel Gottlob Türk
(1756–1813)

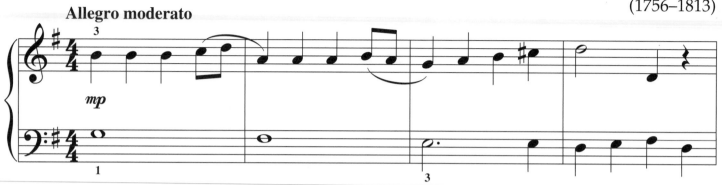

Procession

Alexander Reinagle
(1756–1809)

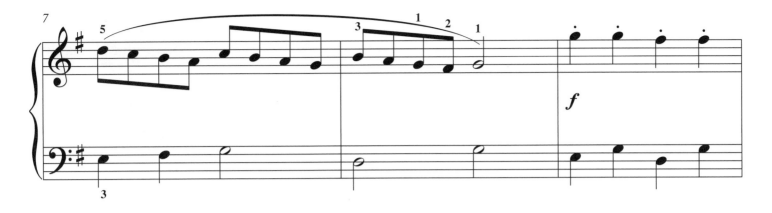

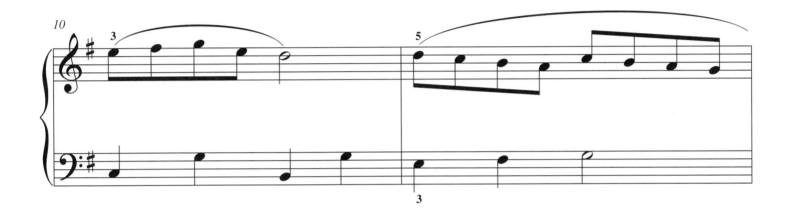

Minuet

Alexander Reinagle
(1756–1809)

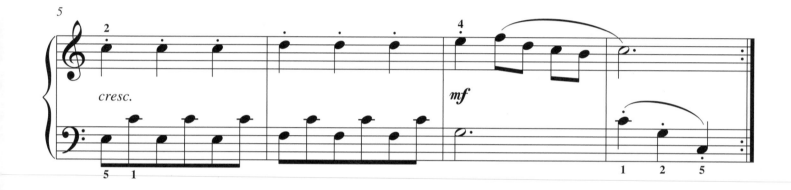

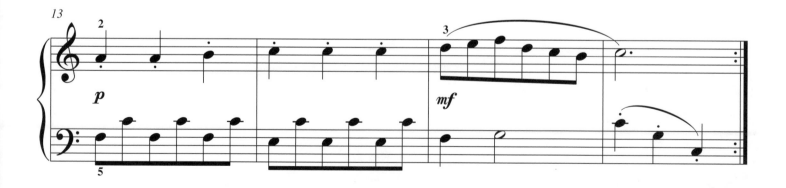

Little Bird
Op. 117, No. 7

Cornelius Gurlitt
(1820–1901)

Melody

Anton Diabelli
(1781–1858)

Moderato

Dance

Cornelius Gurlitt
(1820–1901)

Etude in E Minor
Op. 82, No. 35

Cornelius Gurlitt
(1820-1901)

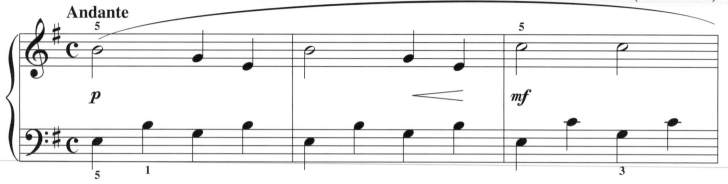

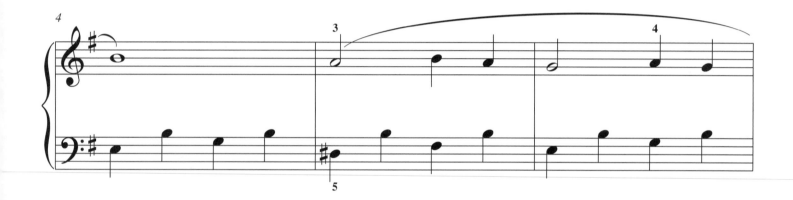

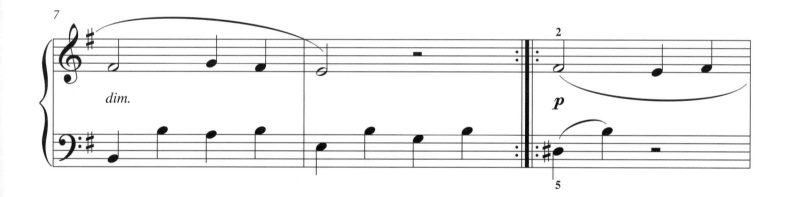

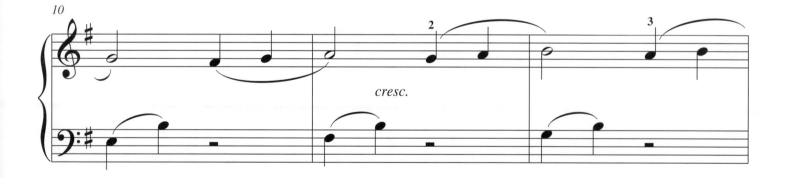

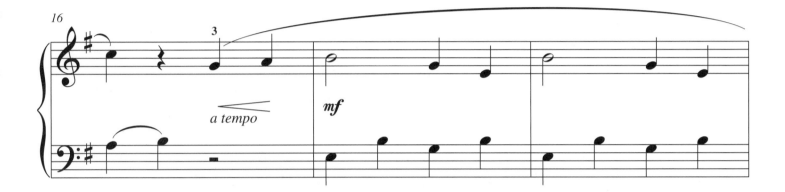

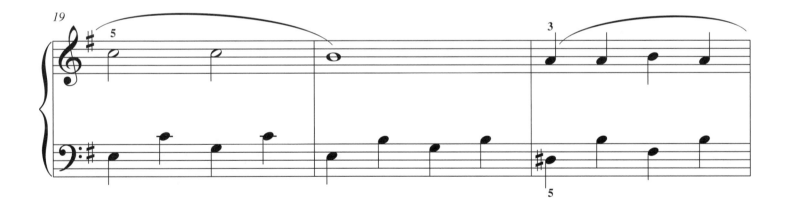

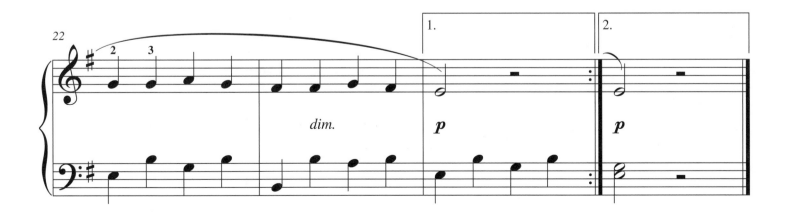

Little Waltz

Cornelius Gurlitt
(1820–1901)

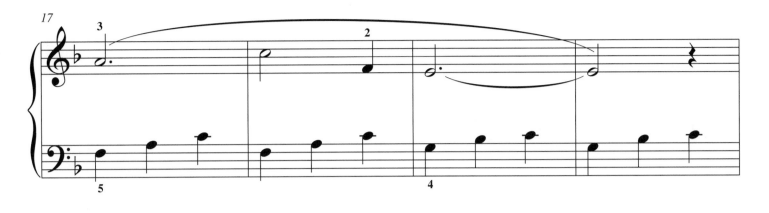

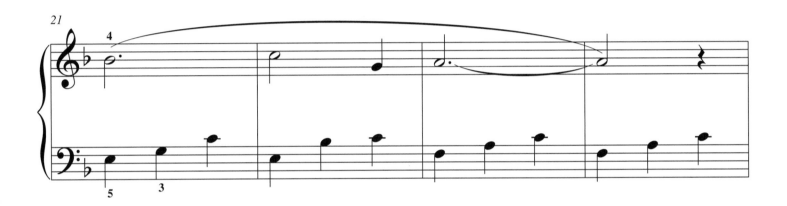

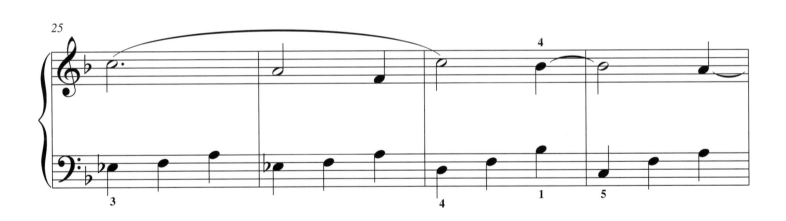

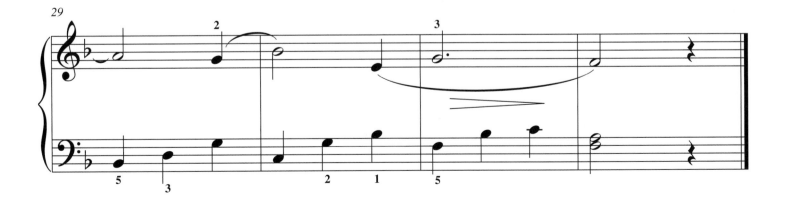

Gavotta
Op. 81, No. 3

James Hook
(1746–1827)

Bagatelle

Anton Diabelli
(1781–1858)

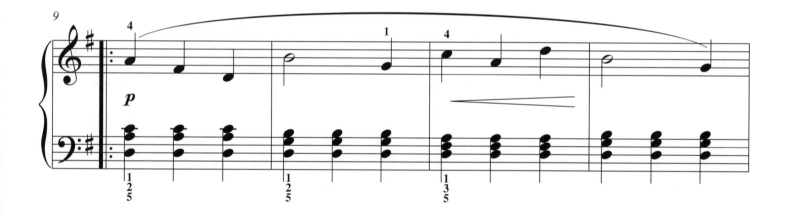

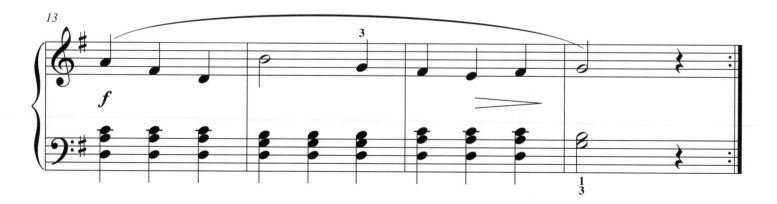

Bourrée in D Minor

Christoph Graupner
(1683–1760)

Moderato

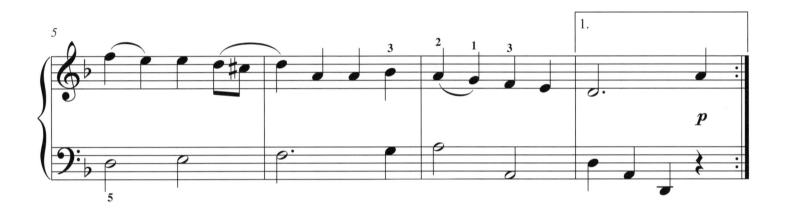

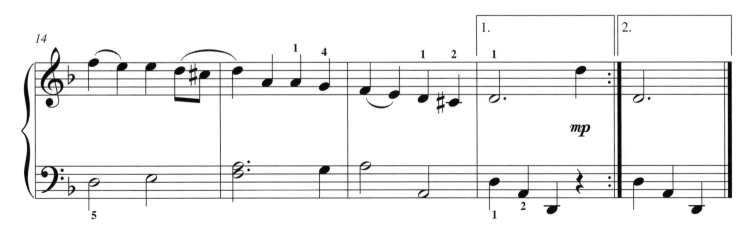

Menuet en Rondeau

Jean-Phillipe Rameau
(1683–1764)

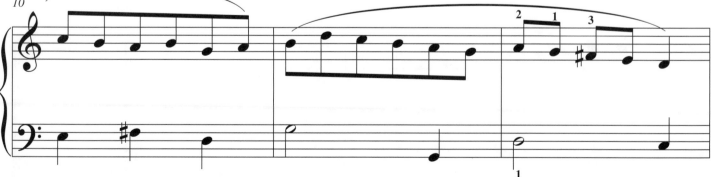

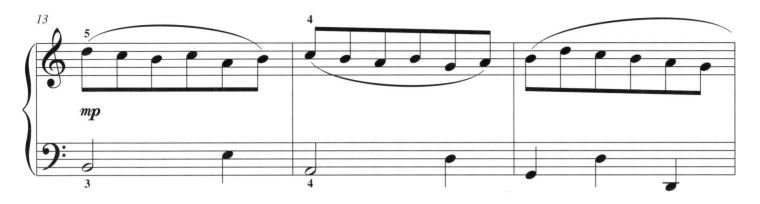

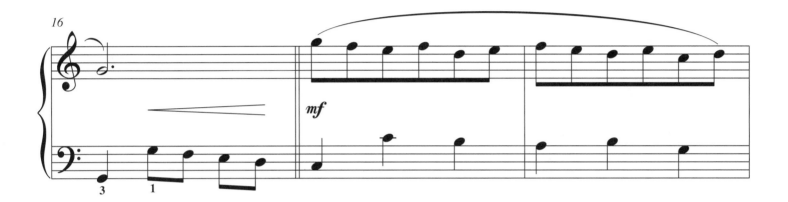

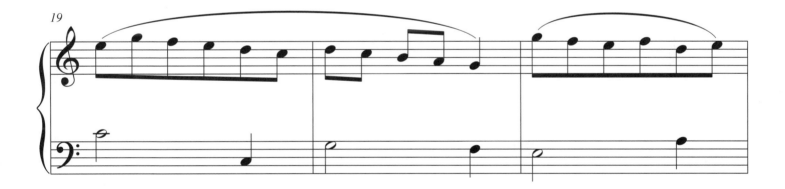

SCHIRMER PERFORMANCE EDITIONS

A CLASSICAL REPERTOIRE SERIES
for the 21st Century

All editions are available with recorded performances. For the newest volumes, the price of the book includes access to online audio files, which may be downloaded. The book/CD packages are being converted to book/online audio access when each volume is up for reprinting.

Visit **www.halleonard.com** to see all titles in the series, including all Beethoven Sonatas as individual editions.

THE BAROQUE ERA
00297067 Early Intermediate............. $9.99
00297068 Intermediate..................... $10.99

THE CLASSICAL ERA
00297071 Early Intermediate............. $9.99
00297072 Intermediate..................... $10.99

THE ROMANTIC ERA
00297075 Early Intermediate............. $9.99
00297076 Intermediate..................... $10.99

J.S. BACH: FIRST LESSONS IN BACH
28 Pieces
00296709 .... $12.99

J.S. BACH: NINETEEN LITTLE PRELUDES
00296786 .... $12.99

J.S. BACH: SELECTIONS FROM THE NOTEBOOK FOR ANNA MAGDALENA BACH
00296589 .... $10.99

J.S. BACH: TWO-PART INVENTIONS
00296463 .... $10.99

BEETHOVEN: EASIER PIANO VARIATIONS
00296892 .... $12.99

BEETHOVEN: FÜR ELISE AND OTHER BAGATELLES
00296707 .... $12.99

BEETHOVEN: PIANO SONATAS, VOLUME I
Nos. 1-15
00296632 Book Only....................... $24.99
00296634 CDs Only (5 Discs).......... $19.99

BEETHOVEN: PIANO SONATAS, VOLUME II
Nos. 16-32
00296633 Book Only....................... $24.99
00296635 CDs Only (5 Discs).......... $19.99

BEETHOVEN: SELECTED PIANO WORKS
00296590 .... $10.99

BEETHOVEN: SIX SELECTED SONATAS
Opus 10, Nos. 1 and 2, Opus 14, Nos. 1 and 2, Opus 78, Opus 79
00296636 .... $18.95

BURGMÜLLER: 25 PROGRESSIVE STUDIES, OPUS 100
00296465 .... $10.99

BURGMÜLLER: 18 CHARACTERISTIC STUDIES, OPUS 109
00296756 .... $12.99

CHOPIN: MAZURKA IN F MINOR, OP. POST.
00296883 .... $8.99

CHOPIN: PRÉLUDES
00296523 .... $12.99

CHOPIN: SELECTED PRELUDES
00296720 .... $10.99

CLEMENTI: SONATINAS, OPUS 36
00296466 .... $10.99

CZERNY: PRACTICAL METHOD FOR BEGINNERS, OP. 599
00296844 .... $12.99

CZERNY: THE SCHOOL OF VELOCITY FOR THE PIANO, OPUS 299
Books 1 and 2
00296899 .... $12.99

CZERNY: THIRTY NEW STUDIES IN TECHNICS, OP. 849
00296874 .... $12.99

DEBUSSY: CHILDREN'S CORNER
00296711 .... $10.99

DEBUSSY: SEVEN FAVORITE PIECES
00296917 .... $12.99

GRIEG: SELECTED LYRIC PIECES
00296886 .... $12.99

GURLITT: ALBUMLEAVES FOR THE YOUNG, OPUS 101
00296619 .... $10.99

HELLER: SELECTED PIANO STUDIES, OPUS 45 & 46
00296587 .... $12.95

KABALEVKSY: 24 PIECES FOR CHILDREN, OPUS 39
00296691 .... $16.99

KABALEVSKY: THIRTY PIECES FOR CHILDREN, OP. 27
00296753 .... $17.99

KABALEVSKY: PIECES FOR CHILDREN, OP. 27 AND 39
00297079 .... $24.99

KUHLAU: SELECTED SONATINAS
00296702 .... $12.99

LISZT: CONSOLATIONS AND LIEBESTRÄUME
00296841 .... $12.99

MENDELSSOHN: SELECTIONS FROM SONGS WITHOUT WORDS
00297080 .... $15.99

MOZART: 15 EASY PIANO PIECES
00296685 .... $10.99

MOZART: 15 INTERMEDIATE PIANO PIECES
00296686 .... $10.99

MOZART: SELECTED VARIATIONS
00296796 .... $12.99

MOZART: SIX VIENNESE SONATINAS
00296785 .... $12.99

MOZART: SONATA IN C MAJOR, K. 545, "SONATA FACILE"
00296705 .... $10.99

PROKOFIEV: MUSIC FOR CHILDREN, OP. 65
00296755 .... $14.99

PROKOFIEV: VISIONS FUGITIVES, OP. 22
00296825 .... $12.99

RACHMANINOFF: PRELUDES, OPUS 3 AND OPUS 23
00296858 .... $15.99

RACHMANINOFF: PRELUDES, OP. 32
00296930 .... $15.99

SATIE: GYMNOPÉDIES AND GNOSSIENNES
00296833 .... $10.99

SCHUBERT: FOUR IMPROMPTUS, D. 899 (0P. 90)
00296700 .... $12.99

SCHUMANN: SCENES FROM CHILDHOOD (KINDERSCENEN), OPUS 15
00296641 .... $10.99

SCHUMANN: SELECTIONS FROM ALBUM FOR THE YOUNG, OPUS 68
00296588 .... $10.99

SONATINA ALBUM
Clementi, Kuhlau, Dussek, and Beethoven
00296639 .... $12.99

TCHAIKOVSKY: ALBUM FOR THE YOUNG, OPUS 39
00296797 .... $12.99

TCHAIKOVSKY: THE NUTCRACKER SUITE, OP. 71A
00296751 .... $12.99

TCHAIKOVSKY: THE SEASONS, OP. 37BIS
00296752 .... $15.99

Prices, contents, and availability subject to change without notice.

G. SCHIRMER, Inc.

FOR MORE INFORMATION, SEE YOUR LOCAL MUSIC DEALER, OR WRITE TO:

7777 W. BLUEMOUND RD. P.O. BOX 13819 MILWAUKEE, WI 53213